Word Bird™

Builds a City

Published in the United States of America by The Child's World®, Inc.
PO Box 326
Chanhassen, MN 55317-0326
800-599-READ
www.childsworld.com

Project Manager Mary Berendes
Editor Katherine Stevenson, Ph.D.
Designer Ian Butterworth

Library of Congress Cataloging-in-Publication Data
Moncure, Jane Belk.
Word Bird builds a city / by Jane Belk Moncure.
p. cm.
Summary: Word Bird builds a city out of blocks,
with streets, houses, stores, and a zoo.
ISBN 1-56766-995-6 (lib. : alk. paper)
[1. Cities and towns—Fiction. 2. Birds—Fiction.]   I. Title.
PZ7.M739 Wn 2002
[E]—dc21
2001006041

Word Bird™

Builds a City

by Jane Belk Moncure

illustrated by Chris McEwan

One day Word Bird said, "I will build a city."

"I need blocks. . .
lots of blocks."

First Word Bird
built roads. . .

lots of roads.

What goes on roads?

Trucks,

cars,

buses,

motorbikes.

What else?

Then Word Bird
built houses. . .

lots of houses.

What goes in a house?

A table,

chairs,

a bed,

lamps.

What else?

Then Word Bird built a school.

What goes in a school?

A chalkboard,

blocks
road
school

desks,

books,

an easel,

paints.

What else?

Then Word Bird
built stores...

18

lots of stores.

What goes in stores?

Cakes,

bread,

cookies,

toys,

ice cream,

cereal,

watermelon,

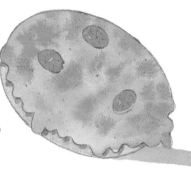

pizza,

pet food.

What else?

Next Word Bird built a zoo

What animals might live in a zoo?

A lion,

a monkey,

an elephant,

a giraffe,

a zebra.

What others?

Then Word Bird built
an airport.

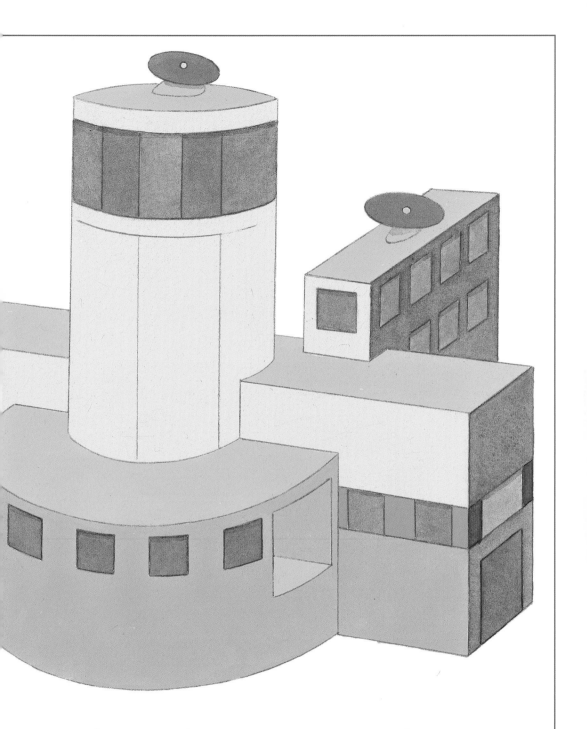

What do airports have?

Passengers,

luggage,

jet planes,

runways.

What else?

Soon Papa came home.
Word Bird said, "I built
a city with blocks. . .

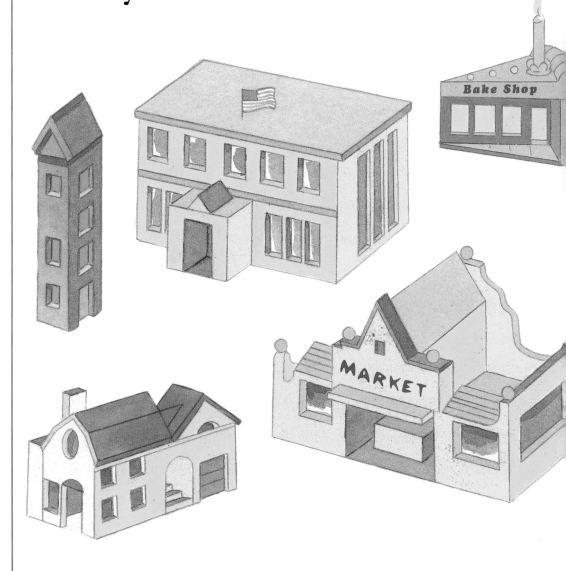

lots of blocks."

Can you read these words with Word Bird?

blocks
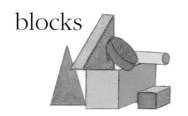

desk

road
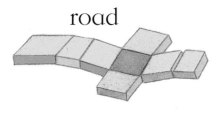

store
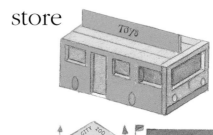

car

zoo

house

airport

bed

city

school

What can you build?